Heartache Poems

Heartache Poems

A Brazilian Gay Man Coming Out from the Closet

Valdeck A. de Jesus

iUniverse, Inc.
New York Lincoln Shanghai

Heartache Poems
A Brazilian Gay Man Coming Out from the Closet

iUniverse, Inc.

For information address:
iUniverse, Inc.
2021 Pine Lake Road, Suite 100
Lincoln, NE 68512
www.iuniverse.com

ISBN: 0-595-33022-3

Printed in the United States of America

Contents

Acknowledgements

To my family:
My dear deceased father, João Alexandre de Jesus, and my dear deceased mother, Paula Almeida de Jesus-who were the most important people in my life.

To my brothers, Valmir, Valdir, Vitório, and Vivaldo Almeida de Jesus.

To my sisters, Valquíria Almeida Guedes, Valdecy, and Ivonete Almeida de Jesus.

To my nephews, Murilo, Rodrigo, Ramon, Roberto Jr., Vítor, and Tiago.

To my nieces, Delma, Jéssica, Amanda, and Paula Fernanda.

To my friends:

Prince Leon A. Kusi (NYC), who told me about iUniverse; Fernando Bingre (Galina Bonanza); Lázaro José (Tia Lau); Ricardo Santana (Dróxina Snydery); Edmar Mascarenhas (Ednéia); Hermano Borges (Molinha); Anderson Menezes (Andreza de Bergerron); Jean (Tieta); Ronaldo Senna; the couple Ivan and Ney; Elias Lima; Elivan José; Joel (Nova Constituinte); Fabrício (my love); Paulo Alberto O. Silva (Nexus 06); Venturine (Itaparica Island); Popoca; Pedrinho (Manuela); Fran; Ito Mendonça; Sivaldo (Policiala); Deinho; Merendinha; Caçula; João de Ascânio; and my friends from Gay Group of Bahia: Cristiano, Denis, Otávio, Ozéas, Cláudio, Luiz Mott, Marcelo Cerqueira.

Special Thanks to:

Gordon Ye (San Francisco-CA), for his helping hand in marketing my book; Ellis Nassour (NYC), for his incentive to keep me writing; Glenn Dessasau (Los Angeles-CA), for his big heart.

Introduction

This book comprises poems about a Brazilian gay man who was born in a small town. The poems explore the obstacles to his acceptance in a conservative society: problems with his catholic family, friends, and neighbors. To try to hide his homosexuality, he dates girls, makes love to them, gets married to one of them, and constantly dissimulates his identity.

These poems reflect his confused personality from that time. Some of them show his points of view about the world's social problems—about prejudice (especially prejudice against gay people)—and others cover a mixture of subjects: religious opinions, hunger, and his protest against everything that is wounding him. Some poems tells about his fear of death and AIDS, although those ideas are not clearly in the texts, but rather in the lines in between.

Trying to hide his sexuality, he writes poems for women when he wants to tell about his romances with men. The poems read like a diary, where he puts everything he can't relate to other human beings. It is a kind of confessional book, and an expression of his heartache and loneliness in the world.

MY DEATH

What kind of cancer will gnaw on me?
How will I rot, still alive?
Will my death be tragic, or will it be comical?
Or will I not even be entitled to a death?
How will I go delirious, or even smile, with a wound swallowing me?
When will I have the pleasure of being strangled by life and death?
Soon I will have the ecstasy of physical paralysis, stuck in a wheelchair….
Amen to that God who perverts and is perverted, who proves to us that we are nothing!
Ugh! Rotten life!

BELOVED

Your face, wrinkled and rough,
With crows feet and acne scars,
Leaves me happy and with an illuminated soul
When I caress it and don't feel anything.

Your body, poorly made and full of blemishes,
Your protruding belly and your crooked legs,
Fill me with peace and pleasure
When I drift away from you, you dead thing.

This, your strange and indifferent look
Fascinates me and drives me wild with pleasure.
The moment in which I feel the greatest joy
Is the one in which I am far from you.

Your presence only annoys and bores me,
For you only drip with perversity.
If you want to see me happy and at peace with myself,
Get away from me, you monstrosity.

KISSING A ROTTEN WOUND

Eating raw banana
I imagine your soul
All dirty and naked.

Climbing a fig tree,
Splintering my lung,
I become dead, dead-alive
Dwelling upon my brother.
Spitting in your mouth,
Drinking all your pus,
I look for life and do not find it.
I look for darkness and do not find it.

I express my anger
Through poetry.
I look for hate and find love,
Find anger and poetry.

Breeding rotten words,
Vomiting filthy feces,
I get all nauseated
And dirty like a pig.

Eating human feces,
Drinking urine and wine,
I die, mad with shame
Shame of dying.

I kill myself with a knife
And have coffee and bread,
Then I live and I am reborn
From the ashes of a volcano.

I grab life and throw it away,
And I pretend to be Jesus,
Drinking fruit punch
Seasoned with my pus.

I call God shameless
And Maria a whore—
All of them big bums
Who always live in struggle.

I throw myself from a high bridge,
Shatter myself on the floor,
I die a cherry virgin,
Because I didn't eat the Devil.

OUR DAILY LIVES

In the horrifying grind
Of each being in the grind,
Lots of pain is experienced,
Destroying our lives,
Preparing us for the fight—
A very unequal fightBetween man and his system.
Voting for dishonest pigs,
Choosing representatives
Who only represent themselves,
Who slip on good meat

Who don't sleep in the drizzle,
But who step on these people,
Alienated and shameless,
Misinformed and without food
For themselves or for their children.
That man who doesn't exist

Or is hidden in the underworld
Of poverty and despair,
That man who takes the bus,
That man who goes to the market,
That illiterate man,
Malnourished and needing affection,
Outcast forced to live like this
By the man in power

Who steps on him and forces him
To suffer for the social good
And forces him to live poorly,
To eat only scraps
Of these leftover exports
That are useless

Except for causing diseases
That kill him without mercy,
Leading him to hell
Without even a notebook
To at least sign his name
And learn how to win in life.

I ADORE YOU

I adore seeing your bulging eyes,
Your face, deformed by blackheads and pimples,
Your nose, big and sprawling,
Which makes your weird face even uglier.

I adore your deformed legs,
Your thighs marked with scars,
Your unkempt arms,
And your uncut nails.

I really like your tangled hair,
Your feet always dirty and bare,
Your skin rough and greasy—
When you touch me, it makes me cringe.

I can no longer live far away from you
Without feeling the stench of your sweat,
Without being pissed off with you,
Talking loudly, with this wildly crowing voice.

POETRY OF SADNESS

Today I received some news
That made me very sad
For it concerned my health
And made me very sad:

Doctor Paulo Sobreira
Examined me and said
That I need to have an operation,
If I like my life,
If I want to live a little more.

He revealed my problem
Without fear of my reaction,
He said that I have a tumor
That will take me to the grave.

I have to leave my job
And whatever worries
To travel to a Capital city
For an operation.

He gave me a maximum of one month
If I want to be hopeful,
For it is a tumor in my intestine,
In either the large or the small.

I became frantic
Because of this news,
But God will help me
Recuperate.

GOD IS NOT GOD. THE DEVIL IS NOT THE DEVIL

Love is not love.
Peace is not peace.
War is not war.
Passion is not passion.
Everything is not everything.
Nothing is nothing.

Beyond everything I want you.
Beyond love I desire you.
Beyond the body I need you.

I love the love that I feel for you.
I feel the peace that is to love you.
I love the anger that I feel for you.
I want you like I want my body.

I desire you like I desire to live;
However, you drift away like a meteor,
Flee like two equal energies,
And forget that my suffering is your suffering.

25-YEARS-OLD

hunger, thirst, lack of affection,
without a home, without a bed, without sentiment,
without school, without medicine, without clothing,
without cologne, without shoes, without a father,
without radio, without TV, without books,
without food, without water, without cover,
without a bicycle, without a motorcycle,
without money,
without anything.
Today I have almost everything,
I'm only missing you, my feminine soul mate,
My masculine soul mate, my heads and my tails,
my lion and my lioness,
to occupy the spiritual vacuum
that grows *ad infinitum* inside of me.

I AM HERE.

I brought everything:
radio, magazines,
pen, paper,
documents,
appointment book, clothes;
everything is here.
Only my soul mate didn't come.
I don't know where she is,
where she goes, and what she does.
I am here:
complete and empty;
broad and restricted;
full and incomplete;
waiting for you
to fill in
the vacuum of my soul.

MY LIFE

I don't want to be sad
I don't want to be sad anymore
But unfortunately I am
I no longer know what to do
To learn English
To learn how to walk
I only know that everything is cloudy
Everything is so dark
That it prevents me from seeing you
I drown myself in tears
Waiting for an exit
Waiting for a solution
But I only see a hole
I only see barriers
Blinding my vision.
But despite everything
Every day I hope
That each day will be better than the previous one
Trying to find the exit
Be it expensive or cheap
That allows me to live
At least one more second
To love my love.

MY LOVE FROM RIO DE JANEIRO

The contact occurs, via satellite.
From phone to phone, a local call,
Conversations, conversations, we agreed,
And the fatal encounter is set.

Time, place, date:
Everything is arranged.
The password will be the following:
"What time is it?"

The correct answer comes:
"The same as always."
Then you crack a smile…

Small talk, beer, looks,
Fatal contact in the field,
And the emotion speaks louder.

MY SELFISHNESS

I never thought you were so cold,
I gave everything of mine to make you happy,
Became two to be only yours,
Stepped on my principles to protect you,
Spent what I could to help you…

And you said that you liked me,
Said that you would go with me to Ilhéus,
Made me think about a life for two,
Made me request a work transfer,
To give you what I didn't have…

And today you trade me for an elementary school,
Say that Bahia isn't a place to live,
Say that you will never return here,
Spitting on the plate that gave you life and love,
Forgetting about the shoulder I offered you.

You don't want me to write to you,
You don't want to call me,
You don't want my visit,
You are ashamed of me.

I only hope that you don't need
To return to Bahia,
For here you found refuge
And, in me, a good friend
Who supported you and gave you affection,
And now you stab me in the back.

But because I like you,
When you are in difficult times,
Look for me urgently,
'Cause I will give you my shoulder,
And I will help you when I can.

VIRTUAL PHONE

Your anguish made me stop
To really reflect about my life:
Whether it was worth it to continue alone,
Suffering, without anyone, in the grind...

Your despair gave me new courage,
Made me dream of being your remedy,
Transforming our life into a dream,
Sending away all that boredom.

I longed to be by your side always,
Loving you, and also being loved,
To stay with you, in every moment,
To have you always by my side.

I slept with you, on my pillow,
I loved you, in my thoughts,
I gave you affection, love and happiness,
I turned our sorrow into happiness...

I stroked your ego, your soul, your being.
I received affection and emotion in return.
I thought about conquering your friendship.
I ended up conquering your heart.

I dream of having your life in mine,
Loving you sincerely,
Being with you always and forever,
With love, affection, and much truth...
(1995, November 30: three days left to meet you).

MY LOVE GEL

To the real illusion:
I don't know if you are a goddess from Olympus,
Resurrected from the abyss,
Or if you are simply a human being,
Born in the Bahian capital;

A well-planned sculpture,
Or an accident that I sculpted;
Ethereal and abstract,
Or concretely real!

Either you are or you are not,
I touched and I felt you—
Felt you tremble with desire...

Whether dream or illusion,
I only know that I remember
Your breathless breathing!

JACOBINA I

Ilhéus awaits me
with open arms.
I don't know whether they are sincere
or whether they are dishonest.
I only know that Ilhéus awaits me
with open arms,
Wanting to squeeze me
with open arms.
I don't know whether they are sincere
of whether they are dishonest.
I only know that Ilhéus awaits me
with open arms.

And there I will be
with open arms,
wanting to hug it
with open arms.
I don't know whether they are sincere
or whether they are dishonest.
I only know that I will go
with open arms.

LOVE WITH THE CITY OF ILHÉUS

(For Greyko, on the trip we took, together, to Ilhéus.)

I arrived here,
And Ilhéus was sleeping,
But its blood circulated,
its veins pulsated, its heart beat,
its brain functioned, silently.
I woke up Ilhéus, made love to Ilhéus,
and I aroused it.
Ilhéus loved me, gave me pleasure, increased my desire,
and exploded in orgasm, together with me.
What a shame I will travel and leave Ilhéus here, in Ilhéus…
If I could, I would move Ilhéus closer to me…

JACOBINA II

I arrived at the finish.
I'm not going to insist anymore.
Sorry for everything.
Don't call me anymore.
Don't look for me anymore.
Don't write to me.
Don't talk to me.
Don't look at me.
I know that you are fed up with me.
It's not my fault that I am how I am.
I'm not going to disrupt you anymore.
I'm not going to call you anymore.
I will no longer take away your peace.
Good-bye!

JACOBINA III

In search of what I feel,
I discovered that what I feel
is strong and is weak,
is large and is small,
is love and is contempt,
is peace and is war,
is *Everything* and at the same time *Nothing*.
I love you, and I repel you.
I seek you, and I drive you away.
because I have you, I love you more.
when I don't have you, I go mad,
but with you I am not sad,
I soon forget about everything.

JACOBINA IV

One more muse,
You are my muse,
my new and confused
conscientious madness,
little one.
What will be that will be born
of this unilateral feeling?
Something beautiful and simple
that will carry me
for a thousand light-years,
or will take me
to the infernal abyss
from which no one returns?

JACOBINA V

Elma Lopes Cajayba
Greyko Santos Silva
Valdeck Almeida de Jesus
Three characters
three actors
three plays
three lives complicated
by the astuteness of destiny
three adults and three children
connected by destiny
Ten points for each one
Zero points for all
How far does one walk?
How far does one fool himself
to live a little longer?

JACOBINA VI

From the top of Cruzeiro Hill, I admire you
I look at your narrow streets
I pass through your mountain ranges with my eyes
and am intoxicated by your rustic beauty

I descend the mountain, hug you
feel your cold soil
the hardness of your stones
and the silence that suffocates you

Only after years on end
do you murmur something
only then do I feel and understand
what your breeze tells me

your streets, your squares
then start to make sense
and I begin to decipher
the feeling hidden inside of you.

JACOBINA VII

Your mouth so coarse, but so attractive...
Your body so young,
Your spirit so advanced (?)...
I beg you with my eyes,
But you don't understand.
Your body so young
but not immature...
I feel your distance
Although now
We split a table
And a beer...
I cannot touch you,
And the only consolation
Is to forget you...

JACOBINA VIII

I sleep alone
With myself, without you
Toss and turn in bed.
I find myself thrown in a corner,
Desiring your smell, your kiss and hug.
I don't find it, and I cling to the dream
Of a day when I can share
My room and my kiss
And all the desire I keep with me…

I LEFT COLLEGE

took slow and rhythmic steps
To look fixedly at nothing
mind far from body
absorbed in daydreams.
        Thinking about you
        pretending to think
        wanting you
        but undecided.
You don't belong to me
I am not your desire
your thinking
is not my thinking.
        I know that I cannot love you.
        I cannot feel this peace
        because this peace doesn't belong to me,
        and I am not entitled to ask you.

THREE CITIES: JEQUIÉ, ILHÉUS, and SALVADOR

Greyko
A friendship/a love
Builds itself/destroys itself
In a century/in a minute

A friend we conquer
A love we buy.

A love betrays itself
And dies for a friend.

MAKING LOVE TO GREYKO

Stage of the first and
of the first and of the first.
Inappropriately proper was the choice:
Also, it would not happen in luxury.
It would have to be there, in the vastness of nature,
That you were built, Jacobina.
It was there that they constructed you: between two
Large stone walls, far from the eyes
Curious about that lonely wanderer
Who follows you.
On the plateau you were the first,
And you will be the first, forever

I RECEIVED A LETTER

And you didn't let me read it.
You tore it up and threw it out
Before I could read it.
You opened the letter,
Didn't read it completely,
Nor let me see it.
Why this attitude?
It was a criminal act!
What happened?
You want me only for yourself,
But you don't want yourself only for me.
Are there no equal rights?

SEPTEMBER SIXTH

A year ago you left;
On September sixth you went away.
You went away forever, to Jacobina.
Elma and I were left with longing.
    I remember, as if it were yesterday:
    Elma and I, taking you to the bus.
    It was 12:15 A.M.: you left,
    And we remained suffering (I, disguised).
I looked to escape from the loneliness.
I looked for replacements,
But you withstand.
The longing never died.

TO SMEARING YOU WITH MY PLEASURE

I lose the will to love,
But my energy rejuvenates itself
When I look at you again.

Then the flame ignites
And invades the mortal spirit,
Makes me hot and wild again.
Then I inject you with the fatal drop.

I fill you up and leave you pregnant,
Like a mare made to give light,
Pregnant with me.

He is born, grows up, and seduces us.
He possesses us and drives us mad,
And we madly climb in the light.

OPPRESSED GOD

This phoney god of the people,
Who kills us with desire,
Is a shameless cuckold,
Bum, and thief;
He's on all sides,
Disrupting the patience,
But was never discovered
By any of the sciences.
He devastates our nation,
Destroys our people,
And afterwards is smiling
From the misery of the people.
He chases me every day,
Runs after me and knocks me down,
Drags me off and drives me crazy,
Inviting me to an orgy.
He never leaves me alone,
Disturbs me everyday,
Driving me to madness
Just to make him happy.
He wants me to get fucked over
And fall into loneliness,
Be stepped on
By all of society,
To fulfill his desire.
But it still didn't work,
And I fear that one day,
When I least expect it,
He will knock me down and tie me up,
Leaving me unconscious
So that he can rape me.
But I won't be in Brazil yet,
But there in another nation,
For before he kills me,
I will kill this thief.
I will drive him wild
And leave him hanging.

DARKNESS

I fled from Earth, riding a slut.
I traveled to Venus, Mars, Uranus, and Neptune.
I had sex with my sister, the goddess of misery
And was reborn from the ashes of Gomorrah

I resurrected the dead and the living,
Rebuilt Babylon and Babel,
Knocked down the Egyptian pyramids,
And diverted the Nile-river-of-honey.
I found refuge in the arms of luxury,
Leaned on the shoulders of Abul,
Took off the pants of the Saint Virgin Slut,
And calmly traveled south.

I returned to the Sun and made my house on it,
Took a ring from Planet Mercury,
Planted banana on the third moon of Uranus.
I plugged up Etna Volcano with chewing gum.

I split Earth in two,
Took the Sea of Fire from Brazil,
Had sex with the lice-infested saints,
Passing through the womb with the Final Judgment.

I herded myself a thousand sheep,
Kept them just within reach,
Left the thousand in search of just one,
Because she was my own mother.

I fled from the fire, and into it I dove,
Found some ice, and in it I buried myself,
Climbed the Andes, and over them I walked,
Pushed myself, and from there I fell.

From the high Andes I took a colossal fall,
Broke apart into shards of grenade,
And after this I was never the same again,
For I was completely whole forever

SAINT WHORE WAR

This war of Saddam
Has surpassed lewdness,
For every day there is war.
But here in my land,
No one takes aim,
Looking like theater
To trick the viewers
Who are watching it.

If I were more cowardly,
I already would have killed him.
I would drive him crazy—
Beyond crazy...naked
To give a little excuse
To all who laugh at him.
And I would even give him a punch
To knock him unconscious.

We already sold many sacks
And all the jugs.
We have no more supplies.
The beans are gone.
So, why more war
If we have no more health
To sell the thieves?

There is a worse war here,
With hunger, plague, and misery,
Something that our politicians
Don't consider as something serious
Because it doesn't create wealth
To fill their large bags,
Which are always empty.

LOST IN THE NIGHT

I wish I could lose myself tonight,
Never again find the road to return,
Be disoriented, dumbfounded, mad,
Indecisive about which route to take.

I wish I could never wake up again,
Be a sleepwalker, wandering in vain,
Run, shout, jump, and fail to find my way out,
Never to wake up from this dream, this illusion

I wish I could fall asleep, forever
In this bed, lost, with you,
Never, ever find the path today,
Lose myself at night, forever with you.

SEARCHING

In the constant search,
Trying to see you,
I find myself and I lose myself,
And I lose you.

I carry this bitterness
of mine,
For I am not capable
Of falling in love with you.

I carry this weight
Of being lonely,
Of conquering no one,
Not even arousing passion.

I am leaving my life
Trying an exit
That gives me a reason
For so much suffering.

If I want, I don't find.
If I find, I hesitate.
If I stay, I hurt myself.
If I run, I don't see…
Where are you, reason to live?

WHO ARE YOU?

I see you in my imagination.
What are you like?
I imagine you as a God-god-God.
Do I want you or reject you?
I don't know whether I love you or hate you.
I love you as a person
I hate you as I hate myself.
I didn't even smile: neither physically nor spiritually,
But I conquered your talking-listening-friend;
I conquered your attention and your look of affection.

GOOD JESUS OF LAPA

In Jequié there are people
Who say they believe in God,
But who are worse than demons
And worse than atheists,
For they kill, curse, and steal,
All in the name of God.

All year-round
They make the world a living hell:
Kill everything that exists
Make the world a living hell
Make the people sad
Make the world a living hell

Kill people and cut people
Shatter the whole world
Dirty themselves and those who are similar
Drag everything away with a rake.
Everything that is very clean
They put in the mud

Pick fights with everyone
Amuse themselves with their acquaintances
Swear and curse
Damn the old days
Undo the true and the beautiful
And murder the unknown.

In August they disguise themselves,
Put on a hat, ribbon, and take food,
Get in their cars and go to Bom Jesus da Lapa
To try to repair life,
To buy forgiveness with money,
Pretending to be forgotten.

Pretending to be forgotten
Some people say they didn't kill,
And if they did it was unintentional.
And even if someone did steal,
Then he is repenting,
Saying that he doesn't remember.

And Saint Idiot forgives,
And the people leave
To kill and to steal
And return later
To plead forgiveness again,
And then turn to leave.

ANXIETY

Now I am alone
Locked in the bedroom
And alone in the world.
I drink beer
Talk to my friends
Take a walk in the city
I read books and newspapers
Do schoolwork
"Amuse" myself plenty,
But I am alone.
I have everything
I am a man
I am not hungry
I can take a bath
I can read and write
I have clothes
I have a job
I have associates and friends
I have my health
I travel for enjoyment
I have my bedroom
I have everything I want,
But I suffer quietly
I suffer alone
In some old corner
Dreaming of love
Loving you in the dream
Having you spiritually
And suffering the anxiety
Of not having you
Loving me here.

LOST

I rot in the demise of the country
Fall apart in broken places
From which I can transcend
And reach human joy.

I realize all of this and suffer
Made a madman who isn't mad,
And at the same time I am consoled,
Thinking that all of this is normal.

What is normal is being unhappy
Or pretending not to be happy,
But this cannot be eternal.

The footsteps leave, and the tracks remain.
Because of this I don't know the path
That I would walk in order to find the exit

CONFUSED

Here and now I desire another,
Another desire that is myself
I, myself, wanting me
Me who is another and nothing
And nothing that is everything
It is everything that is forbidden
It is forbidden to love with truth
With truth, life is feigned
It is feigned because I love myself
Myself I love but I pretend
I pretend not to be foolish
Not to be foolish enough to reveal myself
Reveal myself to myself that here
That here and now I desire another
Another desire that is myself...

CRAZINESS

People are made of clouds
Of clouds, ethereal and fragile
And fragile like great clarity
Great clarity of a fragile life

Great clarity, fragile and ethereal
Ethereal and fragile, great clarity
Disappears as soon as we feel
That they aren't made of clouds.

We look for another cloud
Then, we don't find it, no,
For it dissolves in the great clarity.

Escapes, disappears in the ethereal
In the ethereal illusion
Then, we don't find it, no.

HOW FAR CAN I GO

Deceive myself and others
Without making the mistake
Of empty love?
How long will I go on
Living alone

Looking for the life
That I never lived?

Until I find courage
To seek your lap
Put you in my lap
And be unhappy,
Then I will tell you
A resounding no,
And I will make you feel bad
With my wretched self...

I DON'T WANT TO DIE

How long will death be necessary?
Just step on firm soil.
Step firmly on this ground.
Don't fantasize the real,
For the fall will be fatal.

Don't jump ahead
To arrive, early, at the end,
For the end is only peaceful
For he who "lived" in the middle.

"Better late than never"
For a long time, goes the saying,
And this is very current.

Wait your turn in line
'Cause soon you will reach
The podium that you want so much!

GOD:

is it man or woman?
is it good or bad?
guy or girl?
masculine or feminine homosexual?
Or is it bisexual or hermaphrodite?
I don't know, for I don't know what I am.

I HAVE BEEN LOOKING FOR YOU

For thousands of years
Wanting to find you
To give me peace.
I already went to Easter Island
To the Bermuda Triangle
To Cuzco and Machu Picchu
And to Loch Ness lake.
I also went to Atlantis
Got lost at the bottom of the sea
Looking for you
To be able to love you.
I ask you to listen to my call
And come to find me
For I can't stand it anymore,
To embody and disembody
Trying to find you.

I AM NOTHING

I am the poet of the forbidden.
I am the pastor of the wanderers.
I lead astray he who follows me,
And I pursue peace in this hell.

I am not content with everything.
I am not proud with the whole.
Everything is little for my thirst—
The thirst to expel the peace and quiet of the world.
I am small in the art of love,
But I know how to hate and destroy,
But I know how to end the peace.

I just committed suicide in these words.
I just saw that I am not;
I am not so small after all.

I AM LUCID.

I am dying.
I am conscious
But scared,
Anxious and fearful,
Fearing the future.
And if anyone discovers
that I am dying,
What will I say?

LOVING YOU

I am complete making you happy.
I get happy when I provoke you to laugh.
I get sad if I leave you unhappy.
I get frustrated when I make you suffer.

If I am complete making you happy
If I get happy when I provoke you to laugh
If I get sad when I leave you unhappy
If I get frustrated when I make you suffer,
Then I am selfish
I only think about my well-being
I only want to satisfy my ego,
And I put you down and ignore you
For being complete and individual like you are.

ESCAPING FROM LOVE

Only the mad people can love
Only the mad people are happy
Only, just only, the mad one
Can "slip up."

However, when a clear person slips
Even if he doesn't fall, he is stepped on.
They spit on him, push him
Do everything to see him humiliated.

I already descended the stairs of pride,
But I have to reach the basement.
I know that this is necessary.
But even so, I am not consoled.

I want your chest to rest on.
I want to hear your voice telling me inane things.
I want to be with you in a false life,
Falsely living a "heavy" love.

But all of this is forbidden to me,
I'm not decent enough to dream.
To dream of you is what they allow me,
But to be with you, I can never do again.

ART OF LOVING

art of living
only with the passage of time
do we learn the art of loving
only with the passage of time
do we realize that life is so good
and that time goes by
I can't get over
the "passage" of time,
But I want to live and love.
How do I live and love
if time doesn't pass?
How do I stop the time
to love you for more time?

MY POSTCARD

My postcard is what I see
My tourism is in my bedroom
I live imprisoned by myself
Without wanting to leave from here.

I am imprisoned at this place
Because I am part of here,
And 'cause I adore this heat
And the ingratitude of this land.

I suffer staying here
But I die abandoned,
For I am part of this earth.

My blood runs in the river
My soul lives in the forest
My heart loves the people.

DOING THE SAME THING THEY DID

I walk through paths that I condemned
I love what I rejected
I love risking life
In places never before treaded on.

I cause unforgivable madness
I suffer for being irresponsible,
But I am sorry for everything,
And I would like to be taken higher.

My image doesn't deserve sacrifice
My action doesn't expose me,
But I suffer for being ignorant.

I would like to be in a burrow
Hibernating and dying silently
Than seeing and being scared of facing.

LISBON, MADRID, ROME, NEW YORK

Can you give me peace?
I will look for you soon.
Is there room beneath your bridges
for one more crazy troubadour?

Reserve a park bench for me
Leave a little pollution
Save a rifle shot
Or, who knows, a cannon bullet.

Ensure me the uncertainty of living
Reserve a little loneliness
Save a lack of hope and faith
'Cause I will be your favorite terrorist.

I will blow up bridges and buildings
I will kill innocents and strangers
Only if you give me anonymity
To suffer silently without being bothered.

JOHN LENNON, INDIRA GHANDI, AND I

Were big crazy perverts
Unable to be happy
Despite giving peace to the madmen.

I am a grain lost in immensity
That will never be the first or the last,
For I will always be stepped on and spit on
Like a vermin, crazy and…

CRAZY, I KNOW I AM

But I only want peace
I only look for love
And beyond, nothing more.

Through crooked paths
I look for truth.
I beg the supreme
To give me happiness.

The price doesn't matter
Because I've already paid
Now I want life
To love excessively.

MY DEATH II

I made a date with death.
She didn't appear,
So I thought that she had forgotten me…
I walked, carefree, fearless,
Calmly, fearlessly of being happy.
Then, she took advantage of a moment of carelessness
And set a trap for me.
Put cheese in the mousetrap; Put a worm on the hook;
She did everything.
She succeeded.
She prowled, surrounded, attracted, snatched me completely.
I challenged her, but she was more clever.
I fell into the trap.
The end of a man.
The end of an adventure.

THEY KILLED LIFE

Art imitates life
Life imitates death
And in this complete madness
I live a luckless life.

Running through the forests
Flying through the ground
I find myself fallen and dead
Rotten on the ground.

I open my eyes to life
I see art dying
And history being distorted
While I live life running.

LESS

I cannot be pleased with half. If I could, I would love many people at the same time.
If this is true, I prefer that we forget everything, starting now.
I promise that I won't take away your peace and that, if you want, I will never look for you again.
I don't know to whom I wrote this, nor the date.

MY FRIEND TOLD ME

My friend told me that this city, Jequié, Bahia, is very beautiful. It has wide streets and is full of trees and sidewalks conveniently...it has many pretty things: a river, the one of Contas, with its water that refreshes us from the summer heat.../
...that here there are mountains on every side, that everything is better here, that the air is purer, that the sky is bluer...that the stars shine more for the Jequiens than for any other peoples...that here exist good people that, despite being few, overshadow the evil that is caused by those who aren't good and all the evil that exists in the world...And this friend also told me that all of this is thanks to a very special man: God...

MY CLOSET

When I open you
I see my closet wide open to the world:
Letters, books, poems,
Sadness, and happiness hidden in the corners;
Weaknesses, greatnesses, parts of me;
The smell of mold, cologne, and jealousy;
Everything that makes up my contradicted soul.
I close myself and don't let them see you,
Or get to you, so you don't risk
Becoming the target of the darker ones
And so they don't hurt the feelings I hide in the closet

MAN/WOMAN

Art/life
Tough man/homo-masculine
Everything/nothing
(...)zero/infinity
Beauty/you
I/universe
Here/somewhere
Sound/abysmal silence
Rhythm/(off) cadence
Pity/Cruelty
With you/alone
Point/galaxy
your look attracts me
You drives me wild
I am sad that I don't have you
I am an artist, but I am blind
I don't applaud you, for you deserve more than this.
I want to go to the world of the solitary spirits
To the world of the solitary poets
To the solitary world of the crazy poets.
I love you.

MY (DEFINITIVE) TRIP TO SALVADOR

I'm filled with the juice
Of the juice, of the juice of you
Your sweat is my sweat, your blood runs in my veins.
Your streets are almost my hands.
I want to be a local
I want to breathe your polluted air
I want to exchange fluids
To live your energy
To die in your lap.

MOMENT OF LONELINESS

Every man is alone
He is born alone, lives alone, dies alone
Every man is unique
No one substitutes him
Nothing changes him
Only accidents change
Only accidents alter.
Every man needs affection
Every man needs care
Every man needs love.

Being alone doesn't always mean being lonely;
Being alone is a spiritual state;
Being alone is suffering the drama of living;
Day-to-day, in the cold of a corner;
It is not feeling the touch of someone;
It is not having the moment of shared orgasm.

Every man needs to love
To love every man without fear or terror
Loving a madman with lots of love.

EASTERN EUROPE

The berlin Wall
The Berlin wall
THE BERLIN WALL
the berlin wall

Was built in my chest
Today I am divided
Between Northern love
And Southern love
Eastern (or emotional) love
Western (or rational) love
Accidental (or...) love
Fatal (or trivial) love
I am fighting with myself.

MY FEARS

Fear robs me
Not the fear of dying
But that of prejudice
That of discrimination.

I am not going mad
But it is much worse than this
For I feel it in my skin
And suffer consciously.

It's no use running away
For time is passing
In this hourglass.

I'm disappearing very fast
Dying and walking alive
Pretending not to suffer.

LISTENING TO THE SOUND OF THE UNIVERSE

I see the sword
that wields strong and supreme
I am completely shaken
I give in to this force
Hug the energy
Feel complete in the clouds
Holding your hand
Receiving your force
And all of your happiness
I am large, and I am narrow
I am happy, and I am sad
Not wanting to return again

To the inhumane world
That twists me and suffocates me
Because of this I make a thousand plans
To always be there with you
Diving into this force
That fills my being
And makes me go crazy
Inebriated and dizzy with love.

BROKEN LEG

I want to walk but I cannot
My leg is broken
I only hope that it's brief
For I am sick of lying down
I want to live as a gay
To live the way I am
Showing myself
The monster that hides
Behind the forced smile
And the gesture of friendship.
I want to be complete
And not just one-fifth
I don't want to be an iceberg
I don't want to be an ostrich
But how can I be me in full
After this shell
After this hood
After so much makeup
After so much disguise?
To run far away isn't enough
To stay here doesn't pay
All I have left is certain death
Without living and without dying
Without suffering and without smiling
Just lukewarm water
Just open shade
That doesn't permit viewing
Not even walking
All I have left are false footprints
All I have left is a fake history
And an existence in the darkness
Muffling the feeling
And becoming a rock
Without sense and without destiny.

I WANT YOU

I want myself.
I want myself more than you.
I choose you, and I lose myself.
I lose myself in you.
But when I find you,
I realize that I am in you—
I am you.
So I love myself.

SALVADOR CITY

Hot, Sweaty, Violent, Disturbed,
Agitated, Congested, Filthy, Suburban,
Destroyed, Malnourished, Impoverished,
Touristy, Absurd, Chaotic,
But from another optic,
Pleasant, Heavenly, Demonic,
Brutally obscene
Coherently crazy.

ANOTHER CHANCE

If I had another chance
I don't know what I would do
I think that I already completed
My mission in this life.

The only fear I have
Is the fear of suffering
Suffering before death
And not the fear of dying.

I didn't die from insecticide
I didn't die from appendicitis
For the time never came.

Two motorcycle accidents
Weren't enough,
But this time I won't escape...

IF I SEE YOU

If I see you, I want you
But if I don't see you, I still want
If I escape, I look for you
If I don't find you, I still look.

I desire you completely, completely
I want you completely mine
I desire you completely, completely
To kiss these lips of mine.

I want you completely, completely
Completely, completely for myself
For myself I want you completely.

Never, ever think about me
I want you completely for yourself
And I want you completely here.

WHERE ARE YOU, MY LOVE?

I know that you are there
Somewhere in the world
Waiting for my letter
My affection and my hug
To give you more happiness
And motivation to live
But the lines don't cross
(The two people will never meet)
The roads diverge
Our minds get distracted
Blinding us to the path
Carrying us far away
Destroying destiny
Preventing the meeting
That for us is essential
Leaving us to suffer
Without permitting tranquility
Or a minute of peace.

FEELINGS

I felt my blood boil
And my heart take off
When I was next to you
And could hug you.
        To feel your skin
        To feel your warmth
        I realized that all of that
        Was the purest love.
I kept you in me
With a lot of emotion
I put you in keeping
Inside of my heart.

SEPTEMBER 7TH

Brazilian Independence Day
Liberty Day
But I am crying
Because I am sick
My leg is broken
I cannot walk.
They are going to see the parade.
And I am here lying down.
Everyone getting ready
And I am here lying down,
Made a cripple:
Without the ability to walk.
I am sad and I cry
In this situation.
And wise that I am
That I am just me,
Still, I can't adapt
To this difficult phase
That sometimes frightens me.
My tears fall
Hot like embers
Burning my eyes
And my heart.
My nose clogs
My heart blackens
My mind dies
Killing my dreams.
Days and days are spent sitting
Without walking and without running
But I have faith in my God
That soon I will stand.

MY LIFE II

I suffered through life,
But I was able to conquer
I went hungry for a long time,
And today I can eat.

After so much sacrifice
Of squandering life
When I had to "enjoy" it
Someone cut me short.

I have to interrupt everything
And pursue the uncertain
Before really "living"
But if life wants it so
And there is no other solution
I will leave here shortly...

I AM A POET

I am an imposter
Only I didn't know this:
I am a bad poet
But a great imposter.

I think that I am a poet
But I can only pretend that I am
Poorly pretend that I am a poet
And I trick myself, because I am not a good poet.

I do not know how to make poems
But I love like I desire:
I do everything that I dream.

I am not crazy, but I desire
I find my destiny
That is my boy-heart.

I AM OLD

My thoughts are archaic
My positions are incoherent
My desires are late
My points of view are contradictory
My ideas are subjective
My qualifications are inconclusive
My fights are futureless
My future is the intellectual death…

TO FIND YOU, TO FIND ME

I know your phone number
    But I don't call you
The number of your house
    But I don't write to you
I know where you are
    But I don't look for you
I know where you walk
    But I don't cross your path
I have the tools to capture you
    But I'm scared of what I would do
I know that I want this kind of love
    But I remain stuck in the corral...

YOU

I plan you
I idealize you
I dream of you
I look for you
I fantasize about you
I strive for you
I aspire to make you
I imagine you
I paint you
I sketch you
I project you
I seek you
I invent you
I compose you
I create you
I envision you
I abstract
I daydream you
I visualize you
I foresee you
I anticipate you
(…) you
But I don't prepare myself to correspond
to the highest level of perfection that I expect (or demand) from you.

LONELINESS

There are many lonely people on Earth
people who are lonely and without a friend
because of this I look for a hermit
to be the only one with me

He doesn't need to be ugly
stupid and badly dressed
I just want him to be with me
for the whole life.

LOCK MY HEAD

I am thinking seriously
About quitting the college
For I am bored
Of studying here lying down
Without classmates and a professor
Here in a corner lying down
It is an uncomfortable position
That makes me uncomfortable
Makes me fed up
With everything here
Without the will to study
To do exercises.
But after repenting
I keep thinking
Calculating my loss
If I continue like so.
And I don't know what else to do
If I proceed or if I give up
Could it be that I'm weak
Or does this not matter?
What matters is feeling fine—
Feeling fine with myself.
And I am not relaxed
Not even integrated
In this manner I don't study
Nor do I learn
This is why I'm going to give it some time
I'm going to do the same as some friends
I will return when I can
(And with full energy (?))
To finish satisfying
This important course
That I can't get myself
To continue attending.

THE TRUTH IS BEAUTIFUL

but lying is necessary
To love is beneficial
but to hate is essential
To live is wonderful
but to die is vital
to continue living.

A BODY IS JUST A BODY

A body is not just a body
All physical attraction is just physical
All physical attraction is not just physical
I am attracted by body and by soul
I am attracted just by body
I am attracted just by soul
I like neither body nor soul
I love the spirit, and I hate the body
I love the body, and I hate the spirit
I am fire, and I am water
I am water, and I am fire
I don't like sex, but I like love
I don't like love, but I like sex
Sex just for sex doesn't lift the spirit
Sex just for sex lifts the spirit
I hate falsity, and I love sincerity
I love falsity, and I hate sincerity
I am everything, and I am nothing
I am the Alpha and the Omega; the Beginning and the End;
I am God and the devil. I am and I am not.

CONSCIOUS UTOPIA

Seventy years of revolution
And still I am a radical.
I dream, fantasize, idealize
But I am not capable of making myself happy.
    I cannot make someone else happy
    Nor do I know how to help he who falls
    I am a scientist, and I know everything
    I just don't know why I am here.
At this moment I cannot sleep
For I am in a delightful bed and listening to music;
But I know that someone now sleeps
Under newspapers and on the cold ground.
    I am sad because I have everything
    Or almost everything that I need;
    While someone laughs and sleeps happy
    Supported only by an empty promise…
I go delirious and cry for the inequality of all
Common and humane as anyone
But I know that for spiritual growth
It is necessary to have suffering and displeasure
    Something consoles me and comforts me
    At the same time that it stuns me
    So I spin around like a madman
    Stopped, inert, without being able to interfere.

VERSE AND REVERSE

Coin: heads/tails
sheet: page/verse
man: emotion/pretending
woman: wanting/whatever
sex: active/passive
beauty: esthetic/bias
art: sexless/connectionless
feeling: masculine/feminine
Everything is nothing
                    Act and react
                    Life and relive
                    Who am I?
                    Everything: I am a face
                                        and I have a face
                                        that doesn't put up a face

LIFE

To live I try to,
To die I don't want to;
To smile I wish to,
But I am not able to;
To see myself in you,
I look always;
To love with drive
and with security
I have been trying
since always.
If I cannot
be more authentic,
it is because I am human
And being such, I fail.

YOU ARE UNIQUE

Your eyes are the most gorgeous
as beautiful as the other thousands
as gorgeous as those of all the others.

Your face is the most beautiful and perfect
more beautiful than the face of the most beautiful woman
more perfect and as perfect as the others.

I love you like I love no one
I adore you like a goddess
for you are unique and the same as anyone.

What I feel for you is so big
that it doesn't fit inside of me
as big as a grain of mustard.

YOU ARE NOT A MAN

You satisfy me, but you don't complete me
You are one more thing on my busy agenda
You don't warm me up like my cover does
You are only opium for my pain in uncertain times.

I look for you, and I find you right there
I carry you, and I love you with passion
But I return, and you stay there
Not knowing for sure what it means to live.

YOU, WHOM I LOOK FOR

Have to have:
Sweetness
Sincerity
Unconcern
Patience
Loyalty
Independence
Authenticity
Madness
Energy
Precaution
Conscience
Inexperience
and firm love.

LEAVING

I'm leaving for far away
Far away I will go
I will go to another world
To another better world.

I will return here again
Here I will have to return
I will have to complete the mission
Complete the mission to live.

But I won't ever be the same
The same I will never be
I will never be unhappy.

I will be spiritually poor
But full of purity
And much wisdom.

RUNNING AWAY

I'm going to pay my debts
Free myself from the creditors
To later take a route
Of which I do not know.

I don't want the despair
And I hope to take
Each day with patience
And also with conscience.

I don't want to suffer here
In the eyes of all of you
I will run very far away.

But I am part of this soil
I have roots here
Because of this I am undecided.

THE DAY OF LIGHT—DARK

My day approaches quickly
Like a wolf picking up speed
Wanting to make a surprise
At the most uncertain time.
And I wait for it anxiously
Waiting to see how it is
Dying to feel it in the skin
The sweet/bitter taste of death.
I still haven't even made my grave
But I am on the side of it
Waiting to be pushed.

How much it will cost, I don't know
I only know that I have to pay
For everything that I have left undone.

AND LIFE CONTINUES:

Monotonous, repetitive,
Tedious, routine,
Nothing new, predictable,
Customary, the same "beans and rice."

Nothing is extraordinary, nothing is amazing,
nothing is surprising, nothing is unpredictable…

Everything is mere repetition of already-lived emotions,
if not by you, by other beings…

MARY,

Woman,
Black,
Prostitute,
Illiterate,
Underage,
Poor,
South American,
Northeastern (Brazil),
Ugly,
Physically defected:
ONE HUNDRED PREJUDICES.

I AM MY TWIN BROTHER

I was born prematurely
I lived in the trench of sorrow
I suffered worse than a sufferer
But I am alive to get my revenge.

I am here in the miserable life
That punishes this poor sufferer.
I didn't have a chance to cover what I should
Nor will I have the chance to return...

I don't care about these injustices
For my mission will soon end
I already don't feel the same fear
Not even gossipers can cut me...

I was born a twin of myself
I killed myself, and I am only with me
I don't like to live with this twin
But I tolerate my face day after day.

I suffer daily in my plight
I carry weight beyond my strengths
I look to each day for a little bit of peace,
But what I find is pain and sorrow.

God abandons me every day
Lives each second with me
Follows me and chases forever
And hardly gives freedom of action.

I have pity for this poor man
Who gives into suffering
But there is nothing I can do for him
For he runs away from help. I lament...

Someday I will have peace in my life
Only then will I be able to smile for you,
And on this day maybe I won't exist
And I will be stuck in hell with you...

MY PASSAGE FOR THE EARTH PLANET

What mark will I leave on earth?
What great mark or devastation?
What advanced study or broken record?
What holocaust or aberration?

What mark will i leave on earth?
What great scandal or destruction?
What great agreement or great war?
What great love or betrayal?

What great mark will i leave on earth?
What great mark will i leave on the ground?
Just a great and anonymous mark
Of my passage through this devil-world.

YOU: STAR OF VITÓRIA DA CONQUISTA

The feeling that I fight
The pleasure that I do without
And the same that I look for
When I think about you.

The yearning that I don't feel
The desire to see you
Everything that I deny myself
I want to have with you.

Don't leave me, please
For I want you in abundance
Come to me, my love!

Hug me, kiss me, love me
Make me only yours
Take me all for yourself.

YOU DO NOT LOVE ME

Rapidly
Eluded me
Caused by you and yourself
Awaiting reciprocity, I loved.
Rapidly you knocked me down
Down from the great dream I created:
Of sincere love.

I AM ALONE

At this moment I am alone
Just a point in the universe
Alone and sad
Sad and suffering greatly
Suffering greatly for you
Wanting to have you here
Wishing to forget you
Forgetting you to stop suffering
Suffering for not having you.
At this moment I am alone
I don't know if you are, also
You must be with someone
Talking or making love
And I am here alone
In this immense bedroom...
In this cold and insensitive bedroom...

MY FRIENDS

My job
My motorcycle
My house
My bedroom
My clothes
My videotapes
Everything mine
Except your love
I am unhappy

I WENT TO LOOK FOR YOU

I wanted to make you happy with my presence
But I was just an unwanted surprise
Only after breaking your resistance
Did I succeed in waking us up.

I made you confused, and I planted my seed
Assuming, thus, that I succeeded in balancing you
Then, calmly, to be sure now
I was able to leave without taking you with me.

I await, now, for the plant that I planted
For every fruit to have the taste of honey!
Like they were the kisses that I kissed you.

Anxious, awaiting your response
Unsure of how it will be
If it will be horrible or if it will make me happy.

YOU IN MY DREAMS

(To the *man* that marked my birth into conscious life)

I need to complete myself
To find in you my match
To live with you a love.

Because of this I am struggling
Trying to find you
Wherever I walk.

I feel broken up
Like a man hanged
Without a chance to be happy.

But nothing terrifies me
And I look for you all the time
Trying to find you.

I know that soon I will find you
And I will form with you
A great solution.

Don't try to run away from me
For you will only live
If I make you happy.

YOU HATE ME

I don't wait for you
For I don't want you
I don't see you
But I desire you.

Now I am alone
And you don't want to give me company
I am nostalgic of everything
But you don't even remember anything.

I say: I love you
You say: I'm sorry
I try proximity
But you move away.

I think about you twenty-five hours a day
But you don't even acknowledge my presence.

I only want
Nothing to happen to you
That is happening to me.

RICHARD

I am alone
I am wet from the rain
I am wanting you.

I am crazy
I am insane
I am light
Because I don't have you.

I live anxious
I live obsessed
Crazy for you.

I will die of hunger
I will die of thirst
I will die of nothing
Because I lost you:

I never had you
I never knew you
I never hugged you
Nor kissed you.

I didn't read your letters
I didn't hug you
I also didn't kiss you
And I never saw you...

Alphabetized list

0-595-33022-3